BEGINNING
SIGN
LANGUAGE
SERIES

The
Finger
Alphabet

by S. Harold Collins

Illustrated by Kathy Kifer, Mark Smith and Dahna Solar

Published by:

Garlic Press

100 Hillview Lane #2
Eugene, OR 97401

ISBN 0-931993-46-6
Order Number GP-046

Beginning Sign Language Series

The Finger Alphabet

The Finger Alphabet is the first in our Beginning Sign Language Series. It teaches the manual finger alphabet, the basis for sign language.

Whether a signer is becoming acquainted with the alphabet or whether a signer needs to fingerspell in place of regular signs, **The Finger Alphabet** will be suitable for signers of all ages.

4

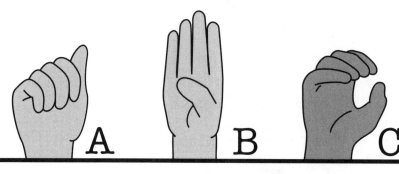 

A   B   C   D

What letters are these?

Draw a line to the letter below.

| D | G | E | A | F | B | H | C |

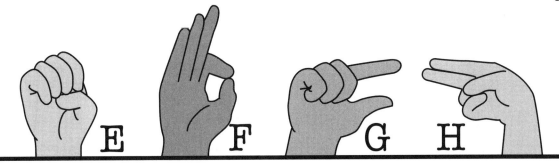

E F G H

Can you identify these words?

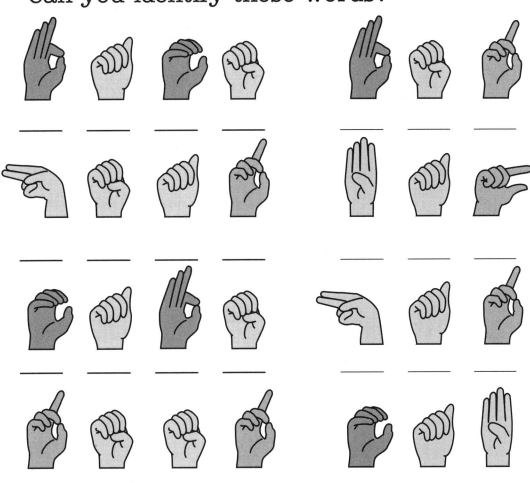

Activity   Practice A to H with a friend. Sign any two letters for a friend
to interpret. Sign two consecutive letters. Your friend follows
with the next two consecutive letters.

I J K L M

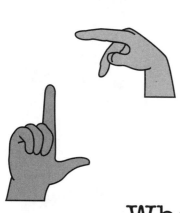

What letters are these?

Draw a line to the letter below.

N Q M P O K L J I

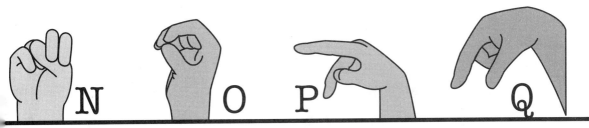

N O P Q

Can you identify these words?

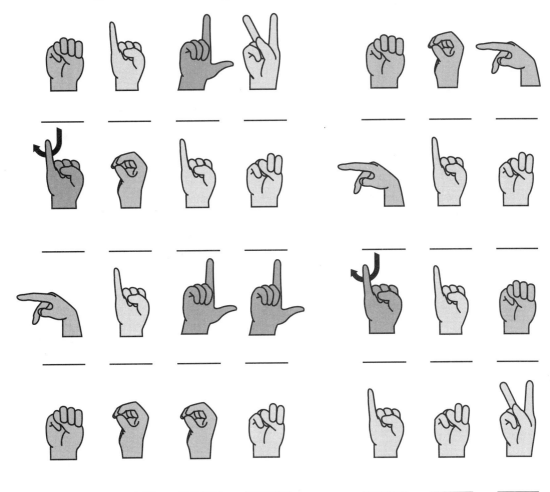

| Activity | Use all the letters you have learned so far. Sign any two letters for a friend to interpret. Sign two consecutive letters. Your friend follows with the next two consecutive letters. |

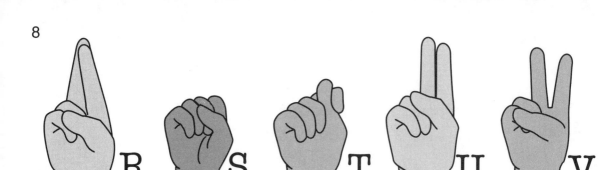

R　　S　　T　　U　　V

What letters are these?

Draw a line to the letter below.

| T | V | R | Z | X | S | W | U | Y |

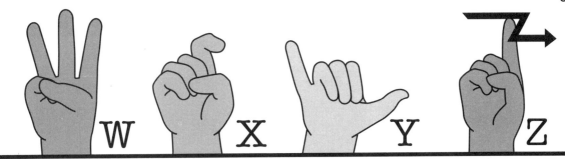

W X Y Z

Can you identify these words?

___ ___ ___ ___   ___ ___ ___

___ ___ ___ ___   ___ ___ ___

___ ___ ___ ___   ___ ___ ___

Activity	You now can fingerspell anything that you can spell. Finger spell your name. Finger spell short words for your friend to interpret.

Connect the dots in alphabetical order to find the hidden picture.

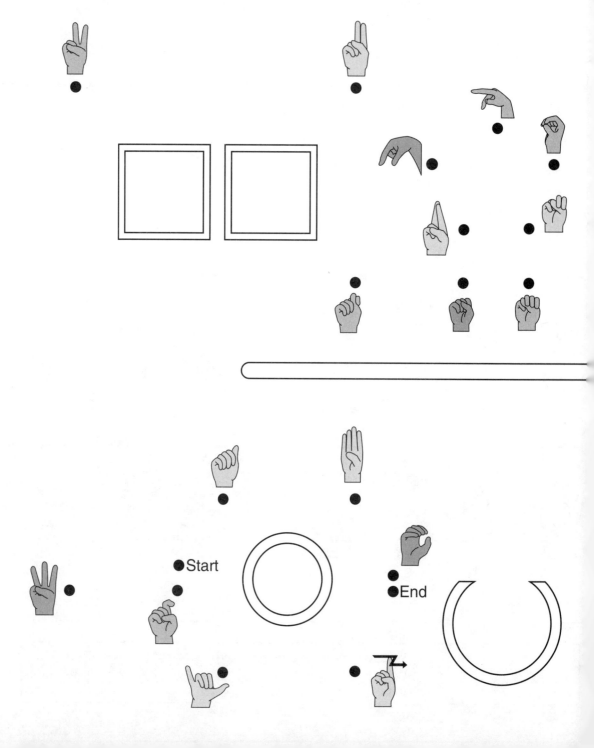

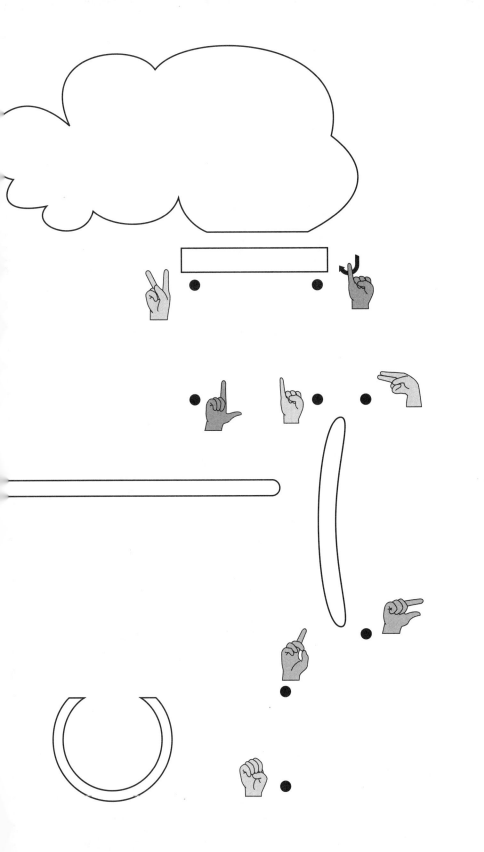

Alphabet Answers

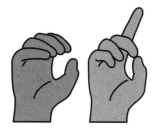 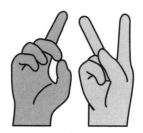 

an insect that stings

a green vegetable

a large body of water

a female sheep

a question asked

myself

opposite of full

having many seeds

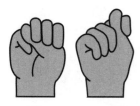

Draw a line to the alphabet letters that answer the descriptions.

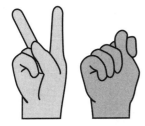

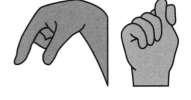

to rot away

a crawling plant

pretty person

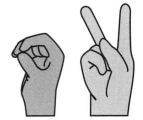

not difficult

all right

jealousy

girl's name

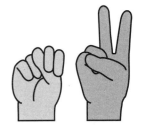

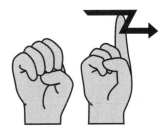

Matching & Decoding

The three alphabet signs on the left have been arranged differently on the right. Draw a line between sign groups which have the same three letters.

Decode these signs. Rewrite the words in alphabetical order.

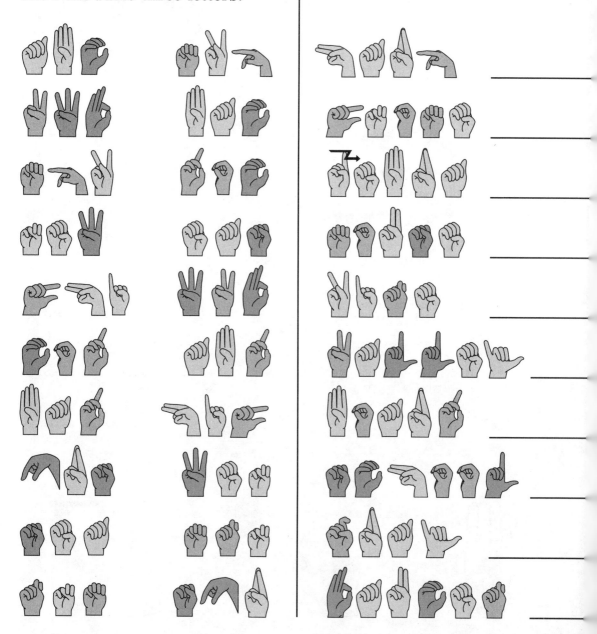

Quick Change

Change one letter in each
word to make it become a fruit.

Change one letter in each
word to make it become
an animal.

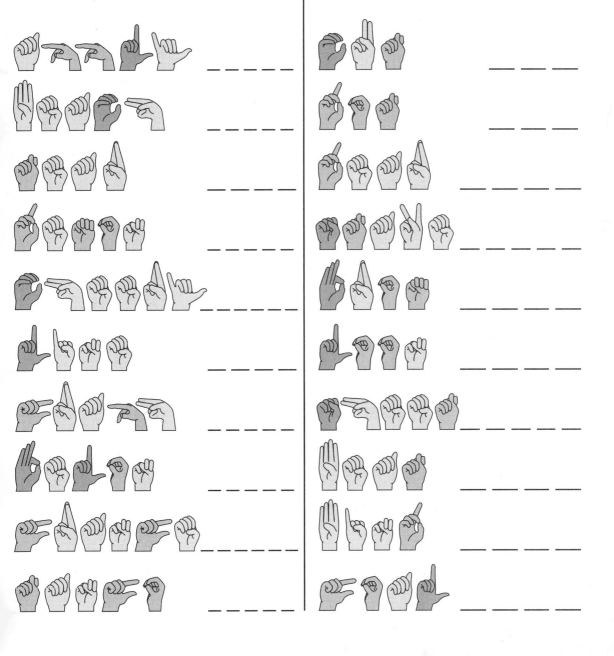

Hidden Pictures

Write the num

1.

2.

3.

4.

5.

6.

7.

8.

9.

10.

11.

12.

13.

e signed word on its hidden picture.

Picture Words
Match the picture with the finger spelling.

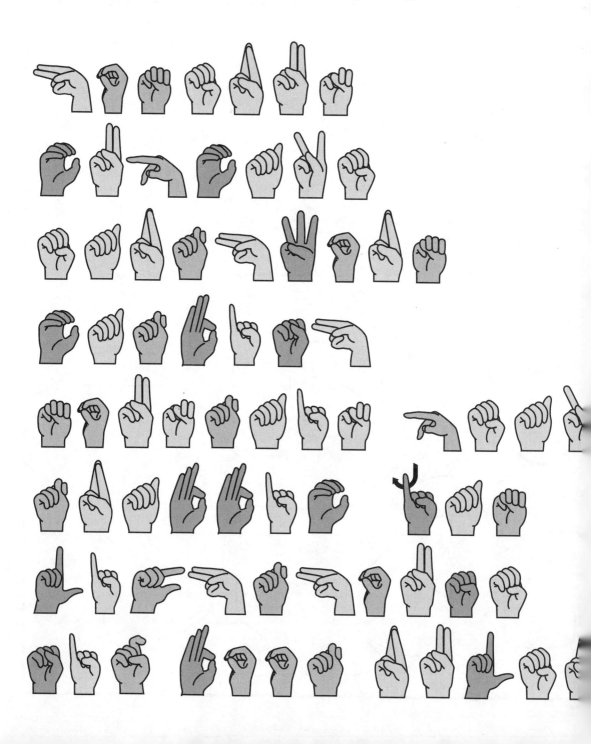

Where in the world?
Draw a line from the country to its name.

Word Search

Find and circle these countries. They are spelled across, up and down, and backward. Four countries are spelled backward.

Canada	Norway	Mali
India	Zaire	Cuba
Spain	Argentina	Peru
Angola	Sudan	Kenya
Italy	Iraq	Chile

Activity

Countries, states, provinces—Fingerspell a country, state, or province to be interpreted.

Or, begin with the letter A. Fingerspell all the countries you can think of beginning with A. Continue on through the alphabet.

Take turns with the same letter or alternate letters with your partner.

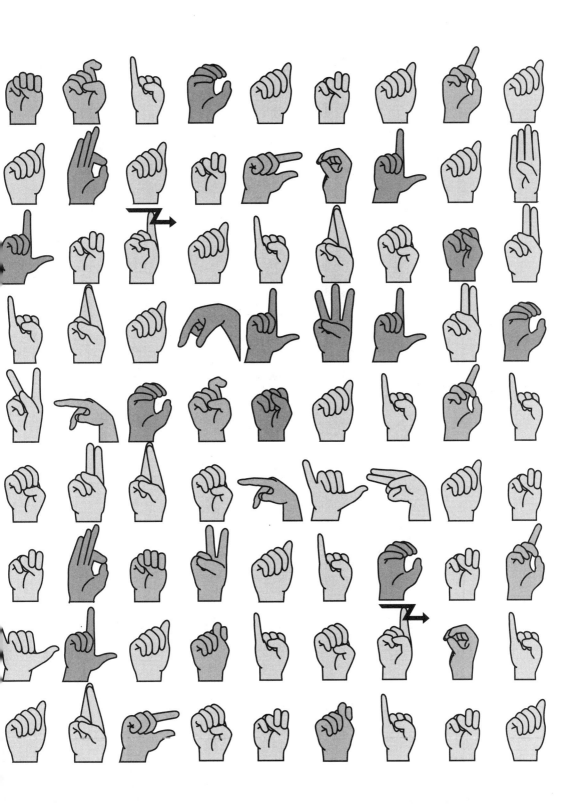

Crossword

Finish this crossword puzzle. All words are pieces of clothing. Missing letters are listed in the finger alphabet. List the clothing after you have placed the missing letters.

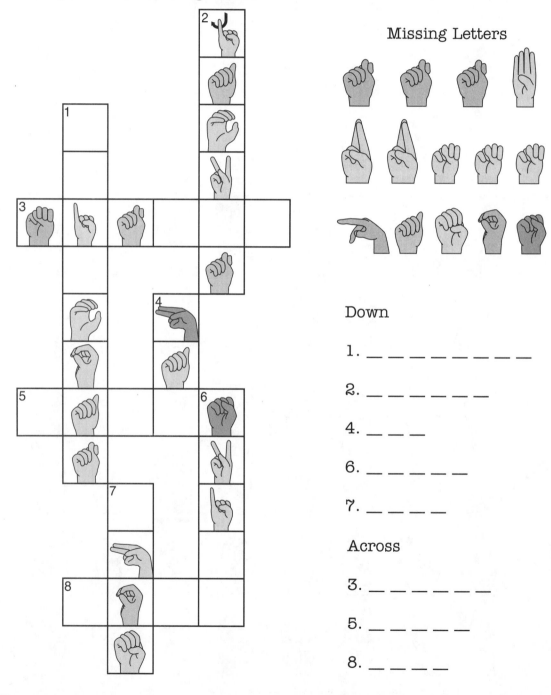

Missing Letters

Down

1. _ _ _ _ _ _ _ _

2. _ _ _ _ _ _

4. _ _ _

6. _ _ _ _ _

7. _ _ _ _

Across

3. _ _ _ _ _ _

5. _ _ _ _

8. _ _ _ _

Unscramble and Rhyme

Unscramble the letters to form words.
Each unscrambled word rhymes with a picture. Draw a line to connect
the word and picture that rhyme.

Answers

Page 4 & 5

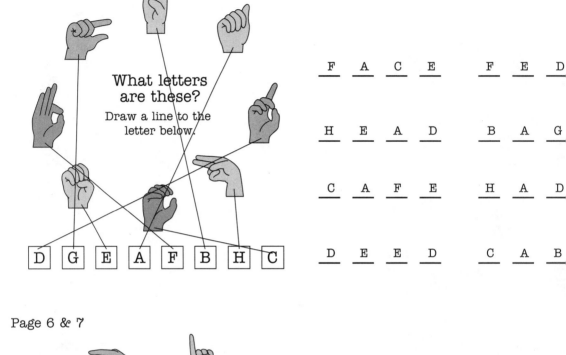

What letters are these?

Draw a line to the letter below.

F A C E   F E D

H E A D   B A G

C A F E   H A D

D E E D   C A B

D G E A F B H C

Page 6 & 7

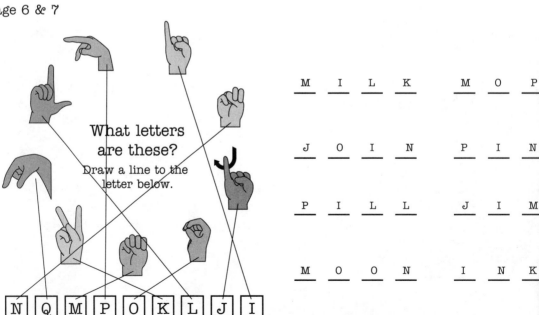

What letters are these?

Draw a line to the letter below.

M I L K   M O P

J O I N   P I N

P I L L   J I M

M O O N   I N K

N Q M P O K L J I

Page 8 & 9

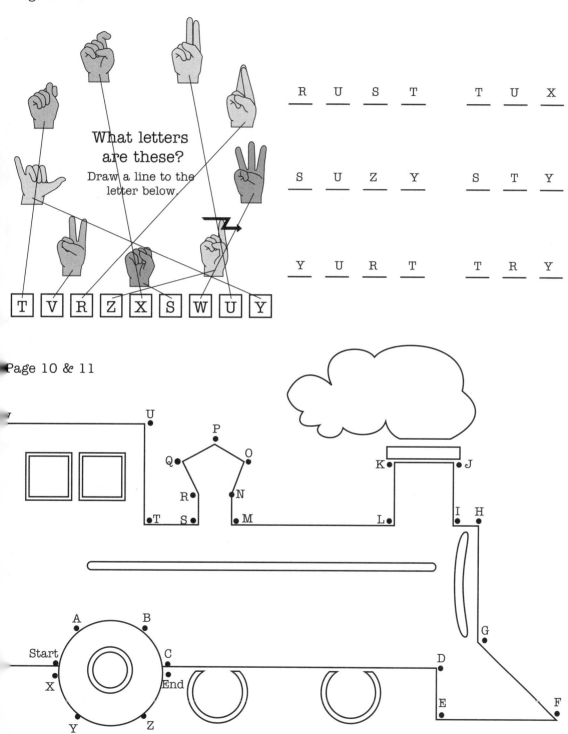

What letters
are these?

Draw a line to the
letter below.

R U S T   T U X

S U Z Y   S T Y

Y U R T   T R Y

T V R Z X S W U Y

Page 10 & 11

Answers

Page 12 & 13, Alphabet Answers

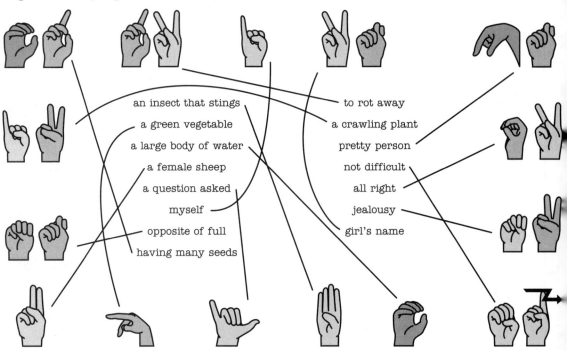

an insect that stings

a green vegetable

a large body of water

a female sheep

a question asked

myself

opposite of full

having many seeds

to rot away

a crawling plant

pretty person

not difficult

all right

jealousy

girl's name

Page 14, Matching and Decoding

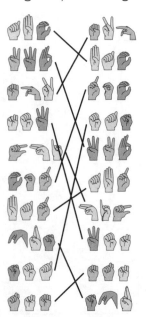

BOARD
FAUCET
GNOME
HARP
KITE
MOUSE
SCHOOL
VALLEY
X RAY
ZEBRA

Page 15, Quick Change

APPLE	CAT
PEACH	DOG
PEAR	DEER
LEMON	SNAKE
CHERRY	FROG
LIME	LION
GRAPE	SHEEP
MELON	BEAR
ORANGE	BIRD
MANGO	GOAT

Page 16 & 17, Hidden Pictures

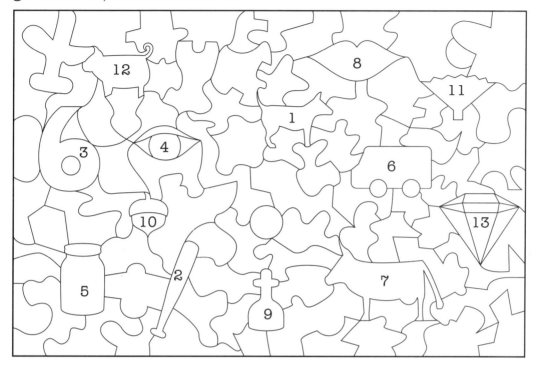

Page 18 & 19, Picture Words

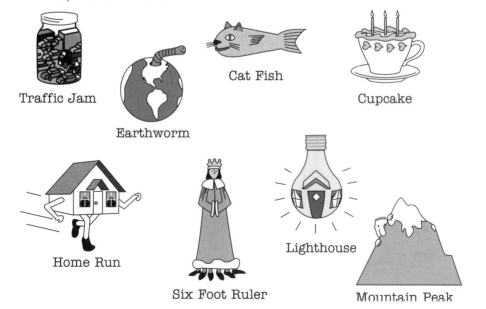

Traffic Jam

Earthworm

Cat Fish

Cupcake

Home Run

Six Foot Ruler

Lighthouse

Mountain Peak

Answers

Page 20 & 21,
Where in the World?

England
France
China
Japan
Mexico
Egypt
Zaire
Brazil
Mozambique
Australia

Page 22 & 23, Word Search

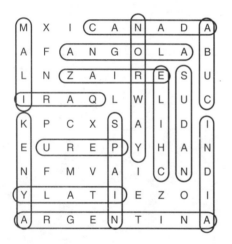

Page 25, Unscramble and Rhyme

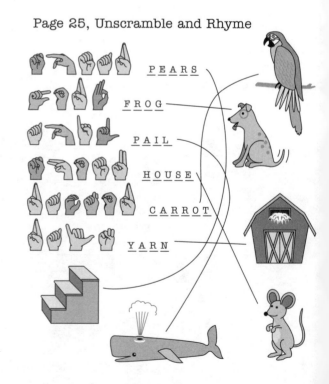

PEARS

FROG

PAIL

HOUSE

CARROT

YARN

Page 24, Crossword

Down

1. RAINCOAT

2. JACKET

4. HAT

6. SKIRT

7. SHOE

Across

3. MITTEN

5. PANTS

8. BOOT